RAILWAY OF HAMPSHIRE AND THE ISLE OF WIGHT

PATRICK BENNETT

AMBERLEY

First published 2023

Amberley Publishing
The Hill, Stroud
Gloucestershire, GL5 4EP

www.amberley-books.com

Copyright © Patrick Bennett, 2023

The right of Patrick Bennett to be identified as
the Author of this work has been asserted in
accordance with the Copyrights, Designs and
Patents Act 1988.

ISBN 978 1 3981 1025 0 (print)
ISBN 978 1 3981 1026 7 (ebook)

British Library Cataloguing in Publication Data.
A catalogue record for this book is available from
the British Library.

Typesetting by SJmagic DESIGN SERVICES, India.
Printed in the UK.

Contents

Introduction

The County of Hampshire saw its first railway with the arrival of the London & Southampton Railway's line from Nine Elms to Winchfield, opened in 1938. This was part of the route from London to Southampton, completed throughout by 1840. Soon to follow were lines to Bournemouth, Portsmouth and Salisbury, built by what had now become the London & South Western Railway. It was clear that Hampshire was going to very much become LSWR home territory. The company did not have it all its own way, however. In the south-east of the county it had a battle with the London Brighton & South Coast Railway, which resulted in the creation of a joint line to Portsmouth. The LBSCR was also to be found running the railway on Hayling Island.

The north of the county was penetrated by four railways running north to south. In the extreme north-east was the South Eastern Railway's line from Reading to Ash. The Berks & Hants, soon to be part of the GWR, built the broad gauge line from Reading to Basingstoke. The Didcot, Newbury & Southampton Railway failed to live up to its name and got only as far as Winchester. It too became part of the GWR. The Midland & South Western Junction Railway ran from Andoversford to Andover. It survived as an independent concern until the Grouping, after which it became part of the GWR. The Isle of Wight ploughed its own furrow; the railways of this small island have a network controlled by no fewer than three different railway companies – a network of which sadly little remains. In 1956 a private company was formed with the object of taking over the Isle of Wight railways. Their plans would have included replacing steam haulage with diesel and reopening closed lines. The then government stated that it had no objection in principle to the takeover but in the event the scheme did not go forward.

The author and publisher would like to thank Peter Lovell for permission to use copyright material in this book. Photographs by the following were used under the Creative Commons Attribution-Share Alike 4.0 License: Geoff Sheppard, Lamberhurst, Ben Brooksbank, Phil Scott, Marcus Giger, and Simon Burchell. Every attempt has been made to seek permission for copyright material used in this book. However, if we have inadvertently used copyright material without permission/acknowledgement we apologise and will make the necessary correction at the first opportunity.

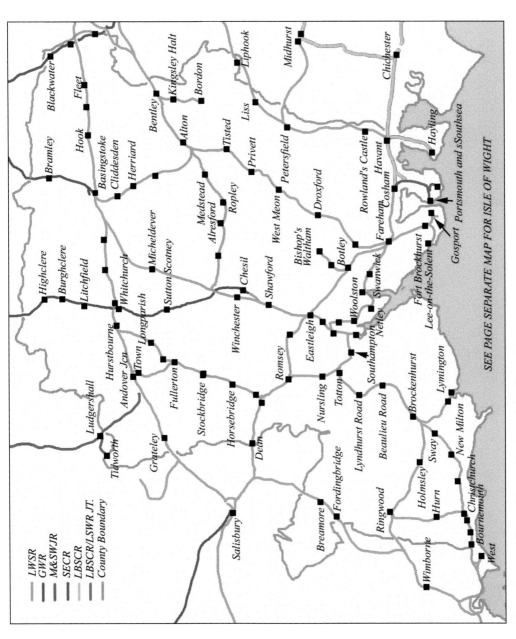

The railways of Hampshire at the time of the Grouping.

The London & Southampton Railway

The London & Southampton Railway was authorised by an Act of 25 July 1834. Progress in building the railway was slow until the first engineer was replaced by Joseph Locke, who employed the contractor Thomas Brassey. By May 1838 construction had reached Woking and public services started. Winchfield was reached in September of that year, while the following year the railway was extended to Basingstoke and the section between Winchester and Southampton completed. The line was opened throughout on 11 May 1840. Winchfield opened as Shapley Heath on 24 September 1838. This is a view of the station from the country end, probably taken around the end of the nineteenth century.

Electro-diesel No. 73109 heads the 06.45 Weymouth Quay–Waterloo boat train at Hartley Witney on 12 August 1983. This would have replaced a Class 33/1 at Bournemouth. (Peter Lovell)

There were originally thirteen stations, fifteen being added later. Gradients were nowhere greater than 1 in 249, the summit of the line being reached at Litchfield, after which gradients were favourable all the way to Southampton. Hook station opened in 1883. In this 1950s view the central island platform is clearly no longer in use. It was later removed.

On 1 July 1961 at Basingstoke, Maunsell 'Schools' Class 4-4-0 No. 30927 *Clifton* waits to leave with the 12.53 stopping train to Waterloo. (Ben Brooksbank)

On the same date, ex-GWR 'Hall' Class 4-6-0 No. 6911 is in charge of a Bournemouth–Sheffield service. It will take the train as far as Banbury. At the time of building its line from Reading, the GWR had its own station at Basingstoke, north of the present one. That station closed in 1932 after which trains used the Southern station. (Ben Brooksbank)

Following the electrification of the Bournemouth line in 1967, Weymouth services were operated with 4 TC units hauled by a Class 33/1 between Weymouth and Bournemouth, where the Class 33/1 would be detached from the rear of the train and an electric 4 REP unit attached to the front. On 4 March 1988 the 07.35 Poole–Waterloo is seen departing from Basingstoke with 4 REP 2007 in the lead. (Peter Lovell)

At Battledown Flyover the LSWR main line splits between the Exeter and Weymouth lines. On 19 April 1984 No. 73125 takes the Weymouth line with a Clapham Junction–Eastleigh ECS working. (Peter Lovell)

Freightliner Class 70 No. 70018 takes the Bournemouth line at Battledown on 2 March 2017 with the 05.36 Garston–Southampton Maritime Container Terminal conveying a range of container sizes. The loading gauge of the line, particularly the tunnel at Southampton, has been continually increased over the years to accommodate larger containers. (Peter Lovell)

GBRf Class 66 No. 66703 passes Roundwood on 8 April 2017 with the 12.02 Mountfield–Southampton Western docks. (Peter Lovell)

Micheldever was one of the original stations on the line, designed by Willam Tite. It was originally called Andover Road; a somewhat optimistic naming since Andover is 13 miles away. The name change came in 1856. The station building is notable for its all-round canopy. It is a listed building, as is the adjacent telephone box.

In 1986 Class 33 No. 33008 was the last Class 33 to receive a classified overhaul under BR ownership and in recognition was repainted in 1960s green livery. On 16 April 1987 it worked a Poole–Leeds relief to Birmingham and is seen later in the day returning through Micheldever with a Carlisle–Poole relief. (Peter Lovell)

Winchester City station in 1955. This was the only settlement of any substance on the line when the railway reached here from Southampton in 1839. It became a through station with the opening of the section to Basingstoke on 30 March 1840.

A double-headed train enters Shawford station. The headcode indicates that this is a service for Bournemouth via Sway. The station was opened on 1 September 1882.

Eastleigh was opened as Bishopstoke in 1839, renamed Bishopstoke Junction in 1852, became Eastleigh and Bishopstoke in 1889, and finally Eastleigh in 1923. On 5 August 1964 Bulleid Light Pacific No. 34092 *City of Wells* stands in the station with a special train for Salisbury. *City of Wells* has been preserved, as have another nineteen of the same class. (Ben Brooksbank)

On 16 August 1966 Class 3H unit No. 1124 stands at Eastleigh with a train for Andover Junction. These units, also known as 'Hampshire Units' and later Class 205, were introduced at the end of the 1950s to work on non-electrified lines on the Southern region. The last ran in 2004.

Nos 33042 and 33112 pass Northam on the outskirts of Southampton with a lightly loaded Willesden–Millbrook Freightliner on 7 June 1986. (Peter Lovell)

This was the original station known simply as Southampton. It had several name changes, the first of these coming when Southampton West was opened. It was later generally referred to as Southampton Terminus. The station building was designed by Sir William Tite and is listed. It closed on 5 September 1966 along with Northam station. Today it is a casino.

In 1847 the arrival of the Southampton & Dorchester Railway brought a second route to Southampton Terminus. In 1858 a curve at Northam was opened to allow London trains to proceed over the S&DR line, thus creating a triangle just south of Northam. At the same time the small station of Blechyden to the west of Southampton tunnel was renamed Southampton West End. A new station further west was constructed in 1892 and this became Southampton West. At the platform of this station stands Midland & South Western Junction Railway Class K 0-6-0 No. 28. This was one of a batch of ten locomotives built for the M&SWJ by Beyer-Peacock between 1899 and 1902. No. 28 was the last built and survived in service until 1937. These were not the only 'foreign' locomotives to find their way to Southampton. Didcot, Newbury & Southampton Railway trains also made their way here.

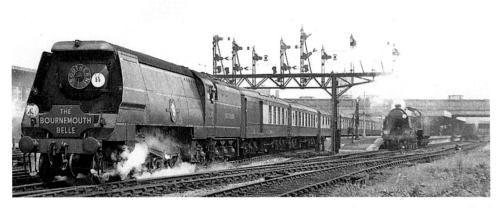

In 1935 the station was renamed Southampton Central. In Southern Railway days Bulleid 'Merchant Navy' Pacific No. 21C16 *Elders Fyffes* pulls away with the Down 'Bournemouth Belle'. The Belle first started running in 1931 as an all Pullman train. It took two hours and nine minutes for the journey, with one stop at Southampton. Before then, from 8 July 1929, the 'Bournemouth Limited' had run non-stop, completing the journey in two hours. This was not the first two-hour non-stop train. In 1911 a two-hour service was put in place contemporary with the introduction of the Drummond 443 Class. The Belle was suspended during the Second World War, resumed in 1947 and ran for the last time in 1967. In 1950 the train reached Southampton in one hour and fifty-eight minutes and Bournemouth in two hours and twenty-two minutes – somewhat slower than forty years previously!

Electro-diesel No. 74003 waits to leave Southampton on 9 September 1977 with the afternoon Weymouth Quay–Waterloo Channel Island boat train. Rebuilt in 1968 from Class 71s, all had been withdrawn by December 1977 and replaced by the smaller Class 73s. (Peter Lovell)

The Royal Pier at Southampton was built in 1833. From 1847 a tramway connected it to Southampton Terminus. In 1871 the tramway was extended along the pier and a station built. The pier was used for the ferry service to the Isle of Wight. In 1909 on weekdays there were seven direct services from Waterloo to the Royal Pier station. The locomotive appears to be a Manning Wardle saddle tank with some kind of condensing apparatus.

Portsmouth

Since 1842 the people of Portsmouth had been able to travel to Gosport by train and from there by ferry to their native city. Clearly this was an unsatisfactory situation and there now followed a struggle between the Brighton & Chichester Railway and the LSWR to provide a direct line to the town. Finally it was agreed that a joint line would be built. The B&C completed the line from Chichester to Portsmouth by November 1841, with the LSWR opening their line from Fareham to Portcreek Junction on 1 October 1848. The joint line was from Portcreek Junction to Portsmouth station. The building seen here in this view taken from the high level platforms dates from 1866. (Geoff Sheppard)

A special train at Portsmouth headed by 'Lord Nelson' Class 4-6-0 No. 860 *Lord Hawke*. No. 860 had been experimentally fitted with a longer boiler to see if this resolved the steaming problems that the class was suffering from. This is possibly a special train to try out the new boiler.

There was a two-platform high level station at Portsmouth from where trains gained access to Portsmouth Harbour station and also to the naval dockyard. In 1955 Adams O2 0-4-4T No. 30207 passes through the high level platforms on its way to the dockyard.

Portsmouth Harbour station opened on 2 October 1876. On 12 August 1940 it was heavily bombed. Four trains were destroyed and one person killed.

Just before Portsmouth Harbour station a line branched off to the north to South Railway Jetty. In 1906 a train stands ready to board troops returning from India.

On 23 April 1992 4-CIG unit No. 1309 passes Fratton Yard with the 08.38 Eastleigh to Portsmouth Harbour. Introduced in 1964, the last of these units was withdrawn in 2005. In 1885 a branch from Fratton to Southsea was opened. It was not a success and closed completely in 1914.

The Portsmouth Direct

While Portsmouth now had a railway station, the route to London was extremely circuitous, so when the Portsmouth Railway Company proposed a line from Godalming via Haslemere to Havant the town was enthusiastically in support. This was the line that became known as the Portsmouth Direct. It was leased by the LSWR and opened fully on 24 January 1859. The first station in Hampshire is Liphook, seen here in the inter-war years before electrification. In 1895 Liphook saw just eight trains a day each way. By 1950 it had a half-hourly service throughout the day. The last train to Portsmouth was at 12.24 p.m. and the last to London at 10.43 p.m.

Petersfield in the 1930s. A view looking south. Today there are just two platforms.

Petersfield became a junction in 1860 with the opening of the branch to Midhurst. The branch closed in 1955. In the nineteenth century Beattie 2-4-0WT No. 191 poses with the branch train. This class of locomotives was extremely long-lived. The last examples, though much rebuilt, lasted until the 1960s. Two have been preserved. The service on the branch in 1909 reflects its rural nature. As well as passenger and goods trains, there was a daily mixed passenger and milk train, with two on Sundays, and a cattle train on Wednesdays if required.

In the early twentieth century the Portsmouth train rolls into Rowlands Castle station behind Drummond T9 Class 4-4-0 No. 337. No. 337 was withdrawn as BR No. 30337 in 1958.

To the north of Rowlands Castle is Woodcroft. At this location during the Second World War a halt was built to serve the nearby Ditcham Park, at the time a convalescent home for sailors. Woodcroft Halt was closed and demolished at the end of the conflict.

The original Havant Halt was to the east of the level crossing at New Lane. The opening of the Portsmouth Direct led to the building of a new station just to the west of the level crossing. The opening of the Hayling Island branch led to a further rebuilding 300 yards to the west. This is the station seen here. The Hayling Island train waits in the bay.

A view taken from the overbridge at the east end of the station in about 1910. The train heading towards the camera is bearing the headcode for the Portsmouth Direct Line. It is being hauled by Drummond K10 4-4-0 No. 386. The tank engine appears to in the process of assembling its train. Its headcode indicates the Midhurst branch.

In the same era, heading for Brighton is Marsh H1 4-4-2 No. 37, later named *Selsey Bill*. The H1 was a class of just five locomotives, introduced in 1905. The last was withdrawn in 1951.

In 1937/8 the station was completely rebuilt in connection with electrification to Portsmouth. During rebuilding work 4-COR 'Nelson' unit No. 3118 passes with a service for Portsmouth.

In the early 1960s A1X 'Terrier' No. 32640 stands in the bay with the Hayling Island 'Billy'. The rebuilt station had two through lines, as well as the platform lines and the bay. (Lamberhurst)

On 26 July 1995 4-VEP (Class 423/1) unit stands at the platform with a Littlehampton–Portsmouth service. The Up through line has already been removed and the Down will follow in 2006. Since this photograph was taken the station has been extensively modified. (Ben Brooksbank)

At Havant on 22 April 2021 unit No. 450 106 forms the rear of the 11.45 Portsmouth Harbour–Waterloo as it takes the Portsmouth direct line. In the distance, Southern Class No. 377 449 approaches on the Coastway Line with the 11.00 Brighton–Portsmouth Harbour. (Peter Lovell)

The Hayling Railway

The Hayling Railway Company was incorporated in 1860. Its plan was to build a line from Havant to South Hayling via Langstone. The greater part of the line would have been built on an embankment across the mudflats to the west of the island. The line was opened for goods as far as Langstone in January 1865. At this point the original plan was abandoned and in 1867 a new Act was obtained authorising a line on a new alignment across land. The 4½-mile railway was finally opened fully in August 1867. There were stations at Langstone and Hayling Island, the latter known as South Hayling between 1869 and 1892. The station is seen during that period with a train hauled by Sharp Stewart 2-4-0 No. 115 *Hayling Island*. This locomotive, together with sister engine No. 270 *Fratton*, worked the line between 1874 and 1889.

From 1872 the railway was leased by the LB&SCR but remained independent until the Grouping. During this period Stroudley A1X 'Terrier' 0-6-0 No. 655 *Stepney* is seen near Langstone. *Stepney* was the first engine acquired by the Bluebell Railway.

The long association of the Terriers with the Hayling Branch was brought about by the insufficiencies of the Langstone Bridge, seen here, as No. 32661 heads southbound. It was the increasingly fragile nature of the bridge that eventually led to the closure of the line in 1962. (Lamberhurst)

This the crossing at Langstone that was never officially authorised. Despite this it remained in use until the line closed. Langstone station is seen beyond the crossing.

In August 1957 A1X 0-6-0 No. 32636 approaches Hayling Island station with a special train. No. 32636 is another Terrier that has been preserved and resides at the Bluebell Railway. (Lamberhurst)

Southampton to Bournemouth

Charles Castleman, a solicitor of Wimborne Minster, proposed a railway line from Southampton to Dorchester via Ringwood and Wimborne. He first approached the LSWR for support but being rebuffed by them turned to the GWR. The GWR were more enthusiastic and put a Bill before Parliament. The Act was obtained on 21 July 1845 but the Railway Board, a Parliamentary committee, decided that the line should be leased to the LSWR rather than the GWR. Its somewhat circuitous route earned it the sobriquet 'Castleman's Corkscrew'. The railway was completed by August 1847. It was double track as far as Redbridge and single thereafter. Within Hampshire there were stations at Blechynden, Redbridge, Lyndhurst, Beaulieu Road, Brockenhurst, Christchurch Road, and Ringwood. Totton was opened as Eling Junction in 1859. In the 1970s a 4-REP unit departs from the station with a service for Weymouth as another arrives.

During 1991/2 D & C tours and Network SouthEast collaborated with a number of Sunday rail tours. On 26 January 1992 Class 56 No. 56019 and Class 33 No. 33114 (providing heating) are seen passing over Redbridge Causeway heading towards Weymouth with the Solent and Wessex Wanderer 4. The train had originally left Waterloo with No. 60086 piloting No. 33114 and at Eastleigh Class 09 No. 09025 took over for a run through the washer plant. On the return, No. 60042 took over at Southampton for the return to Waterloo via Havant and Guildford. (Peter Lovell)

With Sectorisation of BR in the mid-1980s a number of Class 33s transferred to the construction sector and were repainted in its livery. On 17 December 1988 No. 33021 has managed to stray onto passenger duties as it passes Millbrook Freightliner Terminal with the 12.10 Portsmouth Harbour–Salisbury, on this day terminating at Salisbury due to engineering work. (Peter Lovell)

It was the habit of the early railway companies when siting stations nowhere near the communities they were intended to serve to add 'Road' to the name. Anyone getting off at Lyndhurst Road would have found themselves faced with a 3-mile walk to get to the eponymous village. Sensibly, the station was renamed Ashurst New Forest in 1995. In the 1970s a 4-REP unit approaches the station.

Approaching Beaulieu Road station on 19 April 1963 is Maunsell 'N' Class 2-6-0 No. 31821 with the 16.10 Southampton Terminus to Bournemouth Central. The N Class was designed by Maunsell when he was Chief Mechanical Engineer of the South Eastern & Chatham Railway. As well as those built at Ashford, a large number were built at the Woolwich Arsenal under a government contract, and later purchased by the Southern. This led the engines to be familiarly known as 'Woolworths'. (Ben Brooksbank)

Class 47 No. 47447 passes through Beaulieu Road in the New Forest with the 16.42 Poole–Manchester on 24 July 1983. (Peter Lovell)

Near to Brockenhurst a large military hospital was established during the First World War, originally for Indian soldiers, and then between 1916 and 1919 for New Zealanders. Altogether 21,000 casualties were treated there. A train of soldiers due for repatriation departs from the station.

Being the junction for the Corkscrew and Bournemouth Direct lines, as well as the Lymington Branch, Brockenhurst was a busy station, and in 1936 it was enlarged to give two additional platforms. It is seen on 20 April 1963 as Standard Class 5 No. 75663 stands at the platform with the 10.38 Southampton to Bournemouth. The line as far as Bournemouth was electrified in 1967. (Ben Brooksbank)

After several failed attempts the Lymington Railway Company was finally authorised by an Act of 7 July 1856 to build its 4-mile branch from Brockenhurst. The line opened on 12 July 1858 but the town station building, seen here, was not completed until September 1860. In 1879 the company became part of the LSWR. It was this company that extended the line the half-mile to Pier station in order to improve facilities for the Isle of Wight ferries. (Marcus Giger)

When the line was electrified in 1967 it was the last steam-hauled branch on BR. Between 2005 and 2013 the line was operated by two Class 421 units, repainted in 'heritage' colours and named. Unit No. 1498 *Farringdon* is seen at Lymington Pier on 26 May 2005. (Phil Scott)

In the 1960s Standard 3MT 2-6-2T No. 82028 arrives at Holmsley with a service for Bournemouth. Holmsley was originally Christchurch Road. Another very optimistic naming as Christchurch was at least 8 miles away. It was renamed in 1862 following the opening of the Ringwood–Christchurch branch.

At Ringwood Bulleid Light Pacific No. 34006 *Bude* stands with the British Young Travellers Society Hampshire Explorer Railtour. This engine had brought the train from Broadstone, where it is about to return before going on to Southampton. The line from Lymington Junction to Broadstone had closed to passenger traffic on 4 May 1964. West of Ringwood the line remained open for freight traffic but was closed progressively until complete closure in 1977.

The Ringwood, Christchurch & Bournemouth Railway was authorised in 1859 to build a 7¾-mile line from Ringwood to Christchurch. Lord Egton, whose land the line crossed, asked that a private station be provided for his personal use. This was Avon Lodge.

The line opened on 13 November 1862 and was worked from the outset by the LSWR. There was one other station at Herne Bridge, later Herne, and then Hurn. Until the Sway line opened in 1888 this was the main route for trains between London and Bournemouth. After that it became something of a backwater. In 1895 there were six trains daily between Ringwood and Bournemouth East, all of which stopped at Hurn. The line was closed to all traffic on 30 September 1935.

The original Christchurch station, situated some way north of the town. The lines to the left are to Ringwood and those to the right are to Sway. The goods shed is also visible. In 1863 a new Act was obtained authorising the construction of a further 3½ miles to the terminus, which became Bournemouth East, opening on 14 March 1870.

On this 3½-mile stretch there was one intermediate station at Pokesdown. In the 1930s the station was rebuilt to provide four platforms. The station is seen during rebuilding work. A T9 4-4-0 stands at the platform.

In 1947 N15 'King Arthur' Class 4-6-0 No. 749 *Iseult* stands at Pokesdown with a train for Bournemouth West. The two new through roads can be clearly seen. These lines were later removed. No. 749 was withdrawn in 1957 but its name was later carried by Standard 4-6-0 No. 73116.

Boscombe station was opened on 1 June 1897. In the days before the First World War Class H13 railmotor No. 3 stands in the Up platform. Not a great success, all units of this type were withdrawn by 1919.

In BR days LN 'Lord Nelson' Class 4-6-0 No. 30851 *Sir Francis Drake* approaches Boscombe station with a train for Bournemouth. Boscombe station closed in 1965.

The Sway line, linking Brockenhurst and Christchurch, was opened on 6 March 1888. In anticipation of this, a new station at Christchurch was opened to the west of the original station on 30 May 1886. This is the station seen here, photographed in 1986. (Ben Brooksbank)

There were three stations on the Sway, or Bournemouth Direct Line, at Sway, New Milton and Hinton Admiral. A view west from the footbridge of New Milton station in the 1950s.

Bournemouth

Bournemouth West station was opened by the Poole & Bournemouth Railway on 15 June 1874. The Bournemouth Junction Railway linked the West and East stations and a new Bournemouth East station, to the west of the old station, was opened on 20 July 1885. The old East station became a goods depot. Bournemouth East was renamed Bournemouth Central in 1899. In the early years of the twentieth century Adams X2 Class 4-4-0 No. 588 waits to depart with a service for Waterloo.

On 6 June 1960 Drummond Class M7 0-4-4T No. 30105 waits to leave for Bournemouth West with the rear portion of the 10.30 Waterloo to Weymouth. When comparing with the previous photograph it can be seen that the overall roof has been partially removed. (Ben Brooksbank)

Bournemouth locoshed, which was adjacent to Central station, closed with the end of steam on the Southern Region in 1967. On 10 May 1958 Maunsell Q Class 0-6-0 No. 30530 waits for its next turn of duty. (Ben Brooksbank)

At Bournemouth on 27 July 1987 Class 33 No. 33115 has just arrived with the 08.06 Weymouth–Bournemouth service while No. 33102 waits to depart with the 09.28 Bournemouth to Weymouth. (Peter Lovell)

A view of the east end of the station in 1992. A Class 442 waits to depart for London. These units were introduced for the extension of the electrification to Weymouth in 1988. They have now been replaced by newer units and, having no current use, are likely to be scrapped. The roof of the station suffered considerable damage in the Great Storm of 1987 but in 2000 work was done to give the station an overall roof once more.

Bournemouth West was the southern terminus of the Somerset & Dorset Joint Railway. Magnificently turned-out S&DJR 4-4-0 No. 18 waits to depart. No. 18 was built at Derby Works in 1891.

On 23 April 1992 4-VEP unit No. 3529 heads through Branksome Junction en route to Bournemouth. The lines to the right formerly led to Bournemouth West station and now lead to Bournemouth Traction and Rolling Stock Maintenance Depot. Branksome signal box was built in 1886. It retained its original Stephens & Sons thirty-lever frame until closure in 2003, when control of the area passed to Bournemouth.

Eastleigh to Gosport and Beyond

Portsmouth was first reached by way of the railway to Gosport constructed by the LSWR. This 15¾-mile branch from Eastleigh to Gosport via Botley and Fareham opened on 29 November 1841, closed almost immediately due to problems with the tunnel at Fareham, and reopened on 7 February 1842. The journey to Portsmouth was completed by ferry. There were two intermediate stations, at Botley and Fareham. In 1907 a halt was opened north of Fareham to serve the Hampshire County Lunatic Asylum. It closed in 1964. Botley station is seen in the Edwardian period. The Bishop's Waltham branch train is a Class H13 railmotor.

In the early 1860s a group of Southampton businessmen proposed the Bishop's Waltham, Botley & Burlesdon Railway. This would have linked the Peterfield & Midhurst Railway with the Southampton main line. Hostility from the LSWR caused a change of plan and name to the Bishop's Waltham Railway, which would construct a branch from Botley to Bishop's Waltham. The line opened on 1 June 1863. Bishop's Waltham station is seen complete with H12 railmotor No. 1. Designed by Dugald Drummond, this class of just two railmotors appeared in 1904. No. 1 was retired in 1913 and had its engine removed in 1916, thereafter becoming a trailer. The branch closed to passengers in 1932 and to freight in 1962.

In 1947 Drummond 'Black Motor' No. 726 stands at the platform at Fareham with a Gosport–Alton service. Four years after this photo was taken the passenger service was cut to just two return services to Alton daily, and ceased altogether in June 1953.

A view east from the footbridge at Fareham station, taken in 1993, shows clearly how the original station was built to align with the railway to Gosport, seen straight ahead. The Portsmouth lines curve sharply away to the left. Note the 20 mph speed restriction. (Ben Brooksbank)

The magnificent ruins of Gosport station, one of the works of Sir William Tite. The remains have now been converted into a number of residential properties and offices.

In Southern Railway days '700' Class 0-6-0 No. 350 waits to depart with a service to Netley. This class of locomotives was extremely long-lived. Introduced in 1897, the last of the class was not withdrawn until 1962.

The two-road engine shed at Gosport. In the 1930s Class A12 0-4-2 No. 646 passes with the daily goods from Fareham. The shed was demolished by a bomb in December 1940. A new single-road shed was built after the Second World War.

The station was also damaged by enemy action. Incendiaries dropped on 11 March 1941 destroyed the roof and much of the rest of the station. The replacement roof can be seen in this photograph of O2 0-4-4T No. 30200 and the last surviving E1 0-6-0T, No. 32694, in charge of the Solent Limited Railtour that took place on 30 April 1961 and utilised no fewer than six different locomotives.

In 1845 a 600-yard extension as far as the Clarence Victualling Yard was opened. Within the yard a station was constructed for the use of Queen Victoria. The station was adjacent to a landing pier from where the Queen sailed to the Isle of Wight. The Royal Victoria station is seen in a view taken about 1900.

The Victualling Yard was one of many rail-connected facilities used by the Royal Navy. Further north was a connection to Bedenham Royal Navy Armament Depot and Priddy's Yard. This view looking north shows the connection in 1991, shortly before it went out of use. There are no longer tracks here and the trackbed has been turned into a busway.

The Stokes Bay and Isle of Wight Railway & Pier Company received royal assent on 14 August 1855 to build a 1½-mile line from Gosport to a pier at Stokes Bay, from where a ferry would take passengers to the Isle of Wight. The line opened on 6 April 1863. In 1865 a west curve joining the Gosport and Stokes Bay lines was added, making a triangular junction and obviating the need for Stokes Bay trains to reverse at Gosport. At the same time a new station, Gosport Road, was opened at the southern apex of the triangle. In 1909 Stokes Bay had six or seven services daily, including a through train from Waterloo. The ferry service was suspended at the outbreak of the First World War and the train service in 1915. In 1922 the line and pier were sold to the Admiralty. A rare view of a train on the pier, probably dating from the turn of the century.

Fort Brockhurst station was opened on 1 November 1865. In 1950 Drummond L12 4-4-0 No. 30420 arrives at the station. This Eastleigh locomotive had just one more year in service before being withdrawn. Fort Brockhurst closed when passenger services were withdrawn from the Gosport line on 8 June 1953.

Fort Brockhurst became a junction with the opening of the Lee-on-the-Solent line in 1894. This 3-mile railway line was built at the initiative of the Lee-on-Solent Railway Company under the Railway Construction & Facilities Act. There were intermediate halts at Browndown and Privett. The railway was taken over by the LSWR in 1909, who insisted that Privett be renamed Fort Gomer. The initial timetable was of eight returns daily, with three on Sundays. Locomotives were hired from the LSWR, including the 2-4-0T No. 21 *Scott*, seen here at Fort Brockhurst.

At Browndown Halt General Franklin has arrived for a troop inspection. A further halt, Elmore, was opened on 11 April 1910.

The terminus at Lee-on-the-Solent. This was the only station left open after the halts were closed on 1 May 1930 as a money-saving measure. Clearly ineffective as all passenger trains ceased from 1 January the following year.

Goods trains continued until 2 October 1935, when the last train ran, hauled by Stroudley D1 0-4-2 No. 2239.

Eastleigh and Romsey to Salisbury

The line from Eastleigh to Salisbury (Midford) was authorised on 4 July 1844. When it opened on 1 March 1847 it became the main route for trains between London and Salisbury and remained so for the next decade. There were stations at Chandler's Ford, Romsey, Dunbridge, and Dean. Chandlers Ford is seen in the early 1900s. The line curving sharply away to the left led to a brickworks. The station closed in 1969 and the line was singled in 1972. A new station was opened in 2003.

Class 33 No. 33107 arrives at Romsey on 15 June 1985 with the 03.01 Birmingham Curzon Street Southampton, diverted via Andover and Laverstock due to engineering work. (Peter Lovell)

On 29 June 1992 near Awbridge, between Salisbury and Eastleigh, Bulleid Light Pacific No. 34027 *Taw Valley* heads past with a special steam working.

Just inside the Hampshire border Class 33 No. 33015 passes through Dunbridge on 15 June 1985 with the 10.10 Bristol–Portsmouth Harbour. (Peter Lovell)

A train for Salisbury stands at the platform at Dean in the early 1900s.

The line between Romsey and Redbridge formed part of the plans of the Andover & Redbridge Railway (Sprat & Winkle). Before it was completed the line was taken over by the LSWR, opening in 1865. In 1882 a station was opened at Nursling. It closed on 16 September 1957. On the morning of 15 June 1985 No. 33103 passes Nursling with the diverted 08.34 Weymouth–Waterloo. (Peter Lovell)

St Denys to Fareham

The Southampton & Netley Railway was incorporated in 1861 to build a line from Southampton to the Royal Victoria Military Hospital at Netley. It opened on 5 March 1866 but before that time it had been absorbed into the LSWR, which later built the extension to Fareham. This opened in 1889. The Netley line left the main London–Southampton line at St Denys. There were stations at Bitterne, Woolston, Sholing and Netley. Bursledon and Swanwick opened with the extension. Woolston station building, seen here, is in a style typical of Tite. It is listed, together with the rare LSWR type 4 signal box on the platform – although the latter is no longer in use.

The minimal facilities at Sholing. The station is less than a mile from Woolston and when it was opened it was in open country. Today it is subsumed into the vast Southampton conurbation.

The motive behind the construction of the Netley line was to connect Southampton with the military hospital, but it wasn't until 1900 that a branch line was built to the hospital's own station. The 1909 timetable made provision for both ambulance and passenger trains to run to the hospital as required. In front of the looming mass of the hospital Drummond M7 0-4-4T No. 106 stands with an ambulance train.

Hamble station was opened as Hamble Halt in 1942. To the west of the station there is a connection to a branch leading to the Hamble-le-Rice oil terminal, currently disused. On 22 September 1973 the Branch Line Society's Hampshire Branch Lines Railtour included a visit to the branch.

Burlesdon station in 1963. To the east of the station was a branch to a brickworks. This is now the site of the Brickworks Museum. (Ben Brooksbank)

In the late nineteenth century Swanwick was at the centre of the strawberry growing industry. As much as 7,000 tons of fruit was shipped out annually, nearly all by train. Strawberries are still grown in the area but unfortunately they are no longer sent by train. Growers queue up to get their crop loaded onto the train.

Basingstoke to Salisbury

The Act for the line from Worting Junction to Salisbury, the so-called Whitchurch Cut-Off, was passed in 1846. The original intention had been a line from Winchester to Dunbridge, on the Eastleigh–Salisbury line. The slump following the Railway Mania of the 1840s left the LSWR unable to start work on the Whitchurch Cut-Off until the 1850s. Worting Junction to Andover was opened on 3 July 1854 and Andover to Salisbury on 1 May 1857. Drummond T9 4-4-0 No. 285 in as-built condition comes off Battledown Viaduct with a Bournemouth–Waterloo train. The new junction was brought into use on 30 May 1897.

On the new line there were stations at Oakley, Overton, Whitchurch, Andover, Grateley, and Porton. Hurstbourne, seen here, opened in 1882 at the request of the Earl of Portsmouth, who lived at Hurstbourne Park. The station saw a great deal of traffic from the nearby watercress beds but closed in April 1964.

The Class 50s took over the Exeter–Waterloo workings in 1980. On 8 September 1984 Whitchurch station roof was under repair as No. 50040 hurries through with the 09.10 Waterloo–Exeter St Davids. (Peter Lovell)

An early view of Andover station looking towards London.

In the 1980s, Andover still handled fertiliser traffic and was the junction for the branch to Tidworth and Ludgershall of the former M&SWJ line used for military traffic. On 8 September 1984 No. 50006 departs with the 11.10 Waterloo–Exeter St Davids. (Peter Lovell)

A similar view taken on 25 April 1992 as a pair of Class 205 'Thumper' units cross just outside the station.

The reinstatement of the Laverstock curve, just east of Salisbury, enabled both main lines through Hampshire to be used as a diversionary route for the other when engineering work was taking place. On 8 September 1984 Class 33 No. 33026 heads through Andover with the 12.03 Lymington–Waterloo service formed of 4 VEP units. The Class 33 would have been attached at Southampton, where the train would have reversed. (Peter Lovell)

A serious accident occurred at Andover on 6 October 1916 when a fast Up goods ran into a wagon being shunted. No one was seriously hurt but it took three days to clear the wreckage.

Alton and Winchester

The line from Farnham to Alton opened on 28 July 1852. There was an intermediate station at Bentley. This is a view looking west towards the junction with the Bentley & Bordon Railway, which diverged to the left. (Ben Brooksbank)

There were no further developments until the Alton, Alresford & Winchester Railway opened the 17 miles to Winchester on 2 October 1865, by which time it had changed its name to the Mid-Hants Railway. The line was worked from the outset by the LSWR and in 1880 it took a 999-year lease on the line. The view towards London at Alton on 5 February 1955 as M7 0-4-4T No. 30376 stands at the platform with a train for Eastleigh. Note that only the line on the left is electrified. Electrification to Alton arrived in 1937. (Ben Brooksbank)

Medstead opened three years after the other stations on the line. It became Medstead and Four Marks in 1937. In 1999 Ivatt 2MT 2-6-2T No. 41312 runs into Medstead with an Alresford to Alton train. (Ben Brooksbank)

In early Southern Railway days, Adams F6 0-4-4T No. 8 stands at Ropley station. Ropley was famous for its topiary – this remains true to this day.

In 1970 a Class 205 DEMU approaches Alresford station with a westbound service. These units were introduced in 1957, bringing a considerably improved hourly service. By 1970 this was the only passing place on the line. The signalman can be seen waiting to collect the single line token. (John Ragla)

Closure of the line came in 1973 despite a vigorous local campaign. In 1975 the line between Alresford and Alton was purchased by the Winchester & Alton Railway, later to become the Mid-Hants Railway. Trains started running between Alresford and Ropley in 1977, extended to Medstead in 1983, and to Alton in 1985. In the late 1970s sole surviving 'N' Class No. 31874 stands at Alresford.

The Meon Valley

The Meon Valley line was conceived as an alternative route between London and Portsmouth. It had substantial station buildings, 600-feet-long platforms, and the infrastructure was built to accommodate double-track. It opened on 1 June 1903 as a single-track railway and never really progressed to being much more than a branch line, although initially trains ran through from Waterloo to Gosport. The initial timetable had four trains running between Fareham and Waterloo and two from Gosport. On Sundays the two trains ran to/from Portsmouth. A good idea of the substantial nature of the station buildings can be gained from this view of Privett station, taken sometime after closure. (Lamberhurst)

West Meon station shortly after completion.

There were goods stations at Farringdon and Mislingford. In May 1931 a passenger halt was opened at Farringdon. A rather grainy photograph shows the situation in 1955 with the goods shed on the left. After closure to passengers, freight trains continued to run to here until 1968. (Ben Brooksbank)

In the last few years of passenger trains Drummond M7 0-4-4T No. 30055 arrives at Droxford. By this time the service had declined to just four trains daily, with none on Sundays. Passenger services ceased on 5 February 1955 but freight trains continued to run to here from Fareham until June 1962.

A famous meeting
between Churchill,
Eisenhower and others
took place at Droxford on
2 June 1944, just prior to
D-Day. The photograph
was actually taken at
Ascot.

Wickham station. Notice
the station buildings,
identical to those at
the other stations, and
the unusual wooden
footbridge – also
characteristic of the
other stations. In the
left foreground is
the pagoda-shaped
gentlemen's lavatory.

Last train on the Meon
Valley Line waiting to
leave Alton hauled by
M7 0-4-4T No. 30055.
(Ben Brooksbank)

The Basingstoke & Alton Light Railway

The Basingstoke & Alton Light Railway was authorised in 1897, work started in July 1898 and the railway opened on 1 June 1901. There were stations at Bentworth and Lasham, Herriard, and Cliddesden. It is thought that this was the first railway constructed under the 1896 Light Railways Act. Cliddesden is seen shortly after opening.

The railway closed on 30 December 1916, the tracks were lifted and transported to France for use by the army. The line was reluctantly reopened by the Southern Railway on 18 August 1924 but without any passing loops, thus dating this view of Herriard station to the first period of opening.

Bentworth had the same basic facilities as the other stations. The initial timetable was of six passenger trains daily, taking a leisurely forty-five minutes for the 14 miles, as well as a daily goods and a cattle train as required. There were no services on Sundays.

The Bordon Light Railway

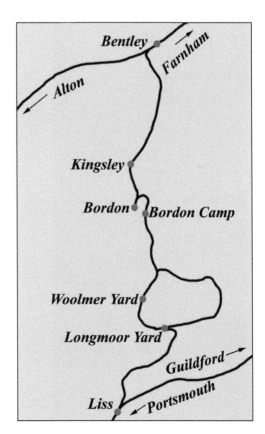

A map showing the layout of the Bordon branch and the Longmoor Military Railway.

At the turn of the century a number of military camps were set up in Hampshire including at Bordon and Longmoor. To serve the needs of the military and provide a service for local people, a 4½-mile light railway from Bentley to Bordon was authorised on 6 October 1902. It was opened on 11 December 1905. An intermediate halt at Kingsley was opened on 7 March 1906. The branch was worked by the LSWR using a variety of tanks for the passenger service including classes O2, T1, D1 and 415. After the Second World War services were worked almost exclusively by Class M7 0-4-4Ts. An 'Ironclad' set at Kingsley Halt on 30 November 1956. The guard appears to be lighting the sole lamp. (Lamberhurst)

The 1909 timetable shows fifteen services daily shuttling back and forth along the branch and on Saturdays there was a through train to and from Waterloo. There were five services on Sundays, the last Down train of the day being a through service from Waterloo. There were two scheduled freight services on weekdays, one originating at Guildford, the other at Farnham. Passenger services ceased in 1957 and complete closure came in 1966. The 'Ironclad' set is seen at Bordon. (Lamberhurst)

In 1905 the military constructed the Woolmer Instructional Military Railway, which ran from the yard at Bordon to Longmoor and included a loop. An extension to Liss on the London Portsmouth line was opened in 1933. The railway was renamed the Longmoor Military Railway in 1935. It too closed in 1966. Seen here is Avonside Engine Company 0-6-0ST 'Woolmer', built in 1910 and now at Milestones Museum, Basingstoke.

The Berks & Hants Railway

There were four railway lines that penetrated Hampshire from the north, all built by railways other than the LSWR. The first of these was the Berks & Hants Railway line from Reading to Basingstoke, opened as a broad gauge line on 1 November 1848. Apart from the GWR station in Basingstoke, which closed in 1932, there was just one station within Hampshire (at Bramley). In 1856 the line was laid to mixed gauge and from 1 April 1869 it became standard gauge only. On 25 April 1992 'Thumper' unit No. 207013 calls at Bramley with a southbound service.

The Reading, Guildford & Reigate Railway

The Reading, Guildford & Reigate Railway opened its line in stages to full opening in October 1849. In 1852 it became part of the South Eastern Railway. There were just three stations in Hampshire, at Blackwater and Camberley (later Blackwater), Farnborough (later Farnborough North), and Aldershot North Camp (later North Camp). This is Blackwater in 1961. (Ben Brooksbank)

The Didcot, Newbury & Southampton Railway

The DN&SR was incorporated on 5 August 1873. It was authorised to build a railway from Didcot to a point 2 miles north of Micheldever on the LSW main line, as well as a branch to East Ilsley and a loop to join the Basingstoke–Salisbury line at Whitchurch. However, nothing happened until the intervention of the Earl of Caernarvon and others in 1879, which led to the first section of railway between Didcot and Newbury opening on 13 April 1882. The railway was worked by the GWR. Ex-GWR Class 2251 0-6-0 No. 3210 stands at Whitchurch Town with a northbound service, sometime in the 1960s. (Lamberhurst)

The DN&S now changed their plans and, despite opposition from the LSWR, gained authorisation in 1882 for a line from Burghclere to the foreshore near the Royal Pier in Southampton. The Act also included provision for a line from Burghclere to Aldermaston. This line was never built. The new line opened to Winchester Cheese Hill on 1 May 1885. At Highclere station on 22 May 1960, Class E1 4-4-0 No. 31067 stands with the North Hampshire Downsman Railtour. (Lamberhurst)

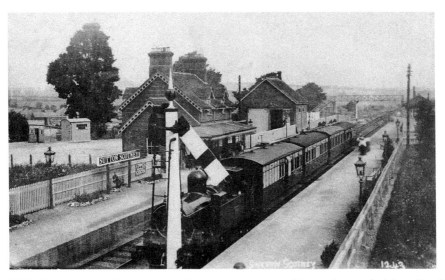

The DN&S later gave up hope of reaching Southampton and instead extended their line from Winchester to Shawford Junction on the LSW line. This extension, always worked by the LSWR, opened on 1 October 1891. In 1895 there were five services each way between Didcot and Southampton, with additional services on Saturdays. There was no Sunday service. In 1909 there were eight services through to Southampton on weekdays and two on Sundays. In the period before the First World War there were through trains from Southampton to Paddington. In the early years of the twentieth century an Armstrong 517 Class 0-6-0 stands at Sutton Scotney with a service for Winchester.

In the 1923 Grouping the DN&S became part of the GWR. During the Second World War the line was of considerable importance particularly in the build up to D-Day. There were as many as 120 movements daily. In 1942 the passenger service was temporarily suspended. In 1943 the line was doubled from Didcot to Newbury and from Enborne Junction to Woodhay. Unusual motive power for a railtour is B4 0-4-0T No. 30096, more normally at work in Southampton Docks – the destination as this railtour waits ready to leave Winchester Chesil. (Lamberhurst)

In 1955 there were five services between Didcot and Newbury and six between Newbury and Winchester. Four of these services ran through from Didcot to Southampton. By this time the Sunday service had been lost. Passenger services south of Newbury ended on 5 March 1960 and north thereof on 10 September 1962. The line was closed completely south of Newbury in 1965 and north of Newbury in 1967. A class often spotted at Winchester Chesil, represented here by Collett '2251' Class 0-6-0 No. 3212 seen in 1957.

Churn station opened 6 July 1888 to serve the nearby rifle range and annual camps on Churn Down. Kingsworthy station opened on 1 February 1909. Soon after opening, a Dean 2-4-0 enters the station.

Pinewood Halt opened on 1 April 1918. It is seen here two years after closure. Note the typical GWR 'pagoda' shelters. (Lamberhurst)

The Midland & South Western Junction Railway

Another line opening in 1882 was the southern section of the Swindon, Marlborough & Andover Railway, later to become part of the Midland & South Western Junction Railway. The only station in Hampshire was at Weyhill. In 1902 a branch was opened from Ludgershall to Tidworth to serve the needs of the War Office. The line was paid for by the War Office and worked by the LSWR. A public passenger service was started soon after opening. Tidworth station is seen in the early years of the twentieth century.

In 1923 the M&SWJR became part of the GWR. The line was very busy during both world wars but after the second conflict went into something of a decline. The line closed completely in 1961 but the section from Andover to Ludgershall was retained for MOD traffic. At Ludgershall station in 1901 stands one of the three Dübs 0-6-0Ts purchased in 1881. These were the first locomotives of the SM&AR.

The Sprat & Winkle

ANDOVER TOWN STATION & MOTOR TRAIN

The Sprat & Winkle started out as a plan by the Andover & Redbridge Railway Company to build a broad gauge line along a derelict canal between those two towns. It was supported by the GWR. The Act was passed in 1858 but little work was done and by 1861 the company was bankrupt. The LSWR was authorised to take over the construction and build a standard gauge line. A single track was completed and the railway opened on 6 March 1865. The route was later realigned and doubled. Andover Town was the northern terminus of the S&W. In the years before the First World War a H13 railmotor enters the station.

At Clatford a Hampshire unit calls in the early 1960s. The V on the unit end was to indicate the brake van end of the unit.

Fullerton had a number of changes. It started out as Fullerton; 'Bridge' was added in 1871, this being changed to 'Junction' in 1885 when the Hurstbourne line was opened before finally reverting to just Fullerton in 1929. Seen at Fullerton on 18 April 1964 is the Hampshire Venturer, organised by the Locomotive Club of Great Britain and headed by Maunsell Q Class 0-6-0 No. 30548. This railtour started at Portsmouth and visited a number of locations in Hampshire before terminating at Southampton. The other locomotive used was USA 0-60T No. 30073.

The Hurstbourne–Fullerton line opened on 1 June 1885. There were intermediate stations at Longparish and Wherwell. Neither Longparish nor Wherwell amounted to very much in terms of population and the passenger timetable reflected this. In 1909 a railmotor provided a service of just five trains daily. There was also a daily goods but no services on Sunday. An early view of Wherwell station.

A goods train running between Fullerton and Longparish continued until 1956. It is seen here at Wherwell in the charge of T9 4-4-0 No. 30288 in the last year of service.

The Salisbury & Dorset Junction Railway

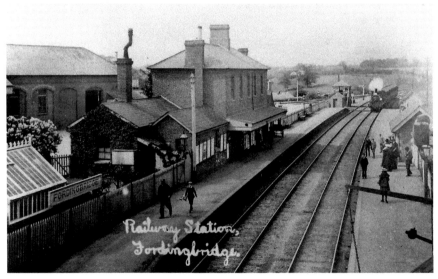

The Salisbury & Dorset Junction Company built the 19-mile line from Salisbury to West Moors, on 'Castleman's Corkscrew'. It opened on 20 December 1866. It was worked by the LSWR and absorbed in 1883. The line followed the valley of the River Avon, weaving in and out of the county. There were just two stations in Hampshire: Fordingbridge and Breamore. Fordingbridge is seen in the early years of the twentieth century as a train for Salisbury arrives at the station. The line closed on 4 May 1964.

The Fawley Line

Despite being authorised as far back as 1903, the line between Totton and Fawley was not opened until the formation of the Southern Railway in 1923. Constructed under a Light Railway Order, the 9-mile line had stations at Marchwood, Hythe and Fawley. Harley Halt opened in 1958 but the railway closed to passengers just eight years later. The line remains in use to serve the oil refinery at Fawley, though now most outward flows are by pipeline, and also for Marchwood Military Port – the line for which branches off to the south of Marchwood station. This is the view north at Marchwood in 1992. The projecting structure on the right is the signal box. Notice the beautiful Southern Railway lamps, now sadly replaced.

Hythe Pier

In 1880 the 700-yard-long Hythe Pier was constructed as a landing stage for the ferry across to Southampton. In 1909 tracks were laid along the pier to be used by hand-propelled trolleys to carry goods and luggage. In 1922 this was converted to an electric railway on the third rail system. Motive power was provided by three Brush locomotives purchased from the Avonmouth Mustard Gas Factory. These were originally battery locomotives but were converted to run on the mains supply. The railway continues to run today, connecting with the half-hourly ferry to Southampton.

Eastleigh Locomotive Depot

The fifteen-road locomotive depot at Eastleigh was opened in 1903. In 1946 it had an allocation of 131 locomotives. It closed with the end of steam on the Southern Region in July 1967. A four-road diesel depot was opened in 1958 to service the diesel-electric multiple units that had recently been introduced. This depot in extended form continues to this day. Its main work is servicing Class 220/1 'Voyagers'. The depot is seen here in Southern Railway days. The line-up includes T9 4-4-0s and O2 0-4-4Ts.

Following Sectorisation it became the practice to stable freight locomotives opposite Eastleigh station rather than at the depot. On Sunday 13 July 1991 Class 47s Nos 47316 and 47277 lead the line-up that includes Classes 33/37/47 and 73. (Peter Lovell)

Eastleigh Works

In 1891 the LSWR carriage sheds and in 1909 the locomotive works were moved from Nine Elms to Eastleigh. Eastleigh became the principal works of the Southern Railway. Construction of new locomotives ended in 1950, but during the 1950s the works was involved in the rebuilding of Bulleid Pacifics. Since Privatisation the works have continued in railway use under private ownership. This aerial view does not include the depot, which is out of shot to the left.

The carriage works seen in the 1920s.

Maunsell's four-cylinder 4-6-0 No. 850 *Lord Nelson* emerged from Eastleigh Works in 1926. At the time it was the most powerful locomotive in Britain. *Lord Nelson* has survived into preservation.

Oliver Bulleid's CC2 was completed in 1945. This Co-Co electric locomotive had a power rating of 1,470 hp. Renumbered 20002 by BR, it is seen here in 1964 at an Eastleigh Works open day. (Ben Brooksbank)

Southampton Docks

The development of the port of Southampton was inextricably linked to the growth of the railway network. By 1876 nearly 10,000 vessels per annum were using the port. Nearly all the freight, as well as passengers, left the port by rail. In 1892 the LSWR bought the docks from the Southampton Dock Company. By the outbreak of the First World War Southampton was the principal ocean passenger port in the country. The Southern Railway continued to develop the docks, which reached their greatest use during the Second World War. The Ocean Passenger Terminal was opened in 1950. It was demolished in 1983.

The 1960s saw the start of the decline, particularly for passenger traffic as flying became the norm for long-distance travel. On the freight side there was a rapid change over to containerisation from the 1970s onwards. There are two rail-connected container terminals in Southampton. The site at Millbrook is mainly used for wagon storage and repair. The Maritime container terminal handles nearly 2 million TEUs per years. Both the Western Docks and the Ocean Dock remain rail connected. (Geoff Sheppard)

In 1903 a trio of B4 0-4-0Ts rest between duties at the Southampton Docks shed. Fourteen of these locomotives were allocated to the docks for shunting. They were later supplemented by LBSCR classes E1, E2 and D1.

After the Second World War the Southern Railway purchased a number of USA S100 tanks for use in the docks. In 1962 the less than entirely successful Class 07 Ruston and Hornsby 0-6-0 diesel shunters were introduced. USA 0-6-0 No. 30072 is seen at Eastleigh Works. (Ben Brooksbank)

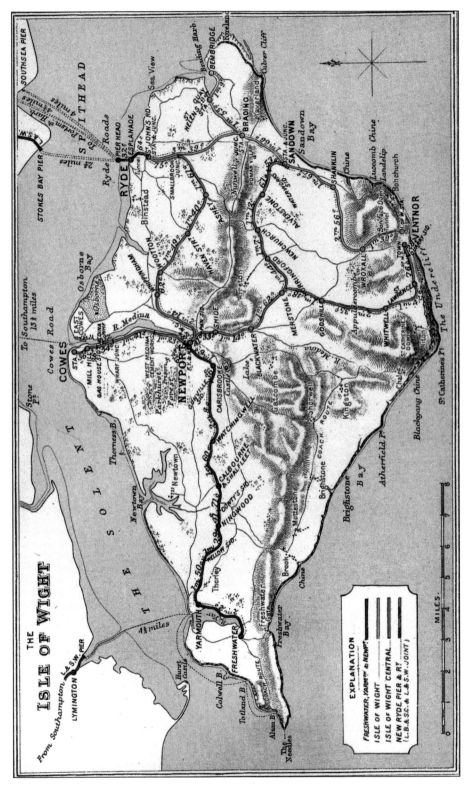

The railways of the Isle of Wight.

The Isle of Wight Central Railway

In 1859 the Cowes & Newport Railway was authorised to build a 4¼-mile single-track railway from Cowes to Newport. It opened on 16 June 1862. There was an intermediate station at Mill Hill, to the north of which was the 198-yard Mill Hill Tunnel. The initial motive power was two 2-2-2 tanks, No. 1 *Pioneer* and No. 2 *Precursor*, built by Slaughter Gunning & Company. These were later joined by an 0-4-2T from Black Hawthorn & Company. In 1908 the IOWC acquired No. 7, a 2-4-0T built by Beyer-Peacock in 1882, from the M&SWJR. It had 5-foot 6-inch driving wheels, the largest of any locomotive to run on the island. It stands at the head of its train at Newport.

The Ryde & Newport Railway, authorised in 1872, opened on 20 December 1875. It used the C&N station at Newport and joined the Isle of Wight Railway at Smallbrook Junction. The two railways were administered by a joint committee. There were stations at Whippingham, Wootton, Haven Street, and Ashey. Ashey Racecourse station was opened later, on the branch from Ashey station, which led to a chalk quarry. Haven Street is seen in the early days of the IOWC.

Whippingham station is less than a mile from Wootton station and remote from any settlement. The only reason it was built was for the convenience of Queen Victoria when staying at Osborne House. Never very busy, it closed on 21 September 1953.

In 1906 the IOWC bought a railmotor from Hawthorn Leslie. In 1913 the locomotive was separated from the carriage and sent to work at Medina Wharf.

The Isle of Wight (Newport Junction) Railway was incorporated in 1868 to build a line from Sandown to Newport. Progress was slow and it was not until 1875 that the railway reached Pan, on the outskirts of Newport. It was to be another four years before the line reached Newport station itself. There were intermediate stations at Alverstone, Horringford, Merstone, Blackwater and Shide. Almost immediately the company went into bankruptcy and from 1880 came under the administration of the C&N/R&N joint committee. In 1887 the three companies amalgamated and took the name the Isle of Wight Central Railway. Sandown to Newport closed on 6 February 1956. A view south at Shide.

In 1889 powers were obtained to build a railway from Merstone to St Lawrence. This was the Merstone, Godshill & St Lawrence Railway. Construction began in 1893 and the line was opened on 26 July 1897. In 1900 the line was extended to Ventnor Town, seen here. The station was later renamed Ventnor West.

Other stations were at Godshill and Whitwell. The railway was worked by the IOWC and absorbed by that company in 1913. The inaugural train of the MGStL stands behind Black Hawthorn 4-4-0T No. 6.

The same locomotive arrives at Whitwell with a service for Ventnor. In 1926 the passing loop and signal box were abolished. The railway beyond Merstone closed in 1953.

The Isle of Wight Railway

The IOW was authorised on 23 July 1860 to build a railway from Ryde to Ventnor. The first 7½ miles from Ryde to Shanklin were opened on 23 August 1864, the final 4 miles following on 15 September 1866. The main engineering feature was the 1,312-yard Ventnor Tunnel through St Boniface Down. There were intermediate stations at Brading, Sandown, Shanklin, and Wroxall. Motive power was in the shape of Beyer-Peacock 2-4-0Ts bought at various times between 1864 and 1883. One of these, No. 14 *Shanklin*, is seen with a Ryde–Ventnor train.

The main locomotive depot for the Island was at Ryde St John's where we see O2 0-4-4T No. 25 *Godshill*. (Ben Brooksbank)

The station at Ryde St John's Road was connected to the pier at Ryde by a tramway, thus entailing a change for passengers making for the ferry to Portsmouth. To avoid this the LBSCR and LSWR jointly provided a line from Ryde to the Pier Head. This opened in 1880 and was used by both the IOW and IOWC. In the 1920s Beyer-Peacock 2-4-0T No. 8 stands at the platform at Ryde Esplanade.

A view of the Esplanade station and pier.

A1X 'Terrier' No. 13 Carisbrooke arrived on the Island in 1927. It is seen here at Brading. It returned to the mainland in 1949 as BR No. 32677.

Under Southern Railway control improvements to the network were made, including doubling between Brading and Sandown. Twenty-three Class O2 0-4-4Ts were transferred to the island and rolling stock was replaced. The inter-war years showed a considerable increase in traffic. In the 1930s at Brading O2 0-4-4T No. 15 has charge of the Ventnor train while another O2 waits to leave with the train for the Bembridge branch. This branch, with an intermediate station at St Helens, had opened in 1882. It closed on 23 September 1953.

Wroxall station is seen in Southern Railway days as a pair of trains cross. The large building on the Up platform is in fact the Station Hotel, which still stands, though now converted to residential accommodation.

In 1864 the first train to Shanklin stands at the platform behind one of the Beyer-Peacock 2-4-0Ts. This machine later had the chimney height reduced and a cab added.

This is the first station at Ventnor. Notice that the LSWR has grabbed the gable end to advertise itself. Not to be outdone, the LBSCR has got itself an equally large sign extolling the virtues of what it laughingly describes as the 'Direct Mid-Sussex Route'.

The station yard was later considerably enlarged and the buildings extended along the platform. One of the Beyer-Peacock tanks has arrived with a service from Ryde.

It was decided to electrify the remaining section between Ryde Pierhead and Shanklin and this was completed in 1967. Ex-London Underground tube stock dating from the 1920s/30s was brought over to work the line. In 1990 these trains were replaced by Class 483 units, also ex-LU trains, dating from 1938. In 2021 the current fleet will be replaced by five two-car Class 484 units. These are ex-LU D78 stock, rebuilt by Vivarail. On 14 September 2021 a Class 483 unit heads along Ryde Pier with a service for Shanklin. (Peter Lovell)

The Freshwater, Yarmouth & Newport Railway

The FY&N was authorised on 26 August 1880 to build a single-track railway between Freshwater and Newport. There were intermediate stations at Carisbrooke, Calbourne, Ningwood and Yarmouth. All but Calbourne had a passing loop. There was additionally the private station of Watchingwell, built for the use of a local MP. This became a public station in 1923. The 12-mile railway was opened to goods on 10 September 1888 and passengers on 20 July the following year. It was worked by the IOWC for 45 per cent of the receipts. An early photograph of one of the IOWC Beyer-Peacocks at Freshwater.

In 1913 the IOWC demanded a greater portion of the gross receipts for working the line. This being unacceptable, the FY&N decided to work the line themselves and in doing so almost immediately became bankrupt. With external help the railway was able to obtain locomotives and rolling stock and continue operating. Hitherto the railway had used the IOWC Newport station, something they were no longer able to do. Consequently it was necessary to build their own station in Newport, some distance from that of the IOWC, with all the inconvenience that involved for passengers changing trains. The FY&N obtained two locomotives: No. 1 *Medina*, a Manning Wardle saddle tank of 1913 vintage, and A1 'Terrier' No. 2 *Freshwater*, formerly LBSCR No. 646 *Newington*. Rolling stock was obtained from the Manchester South Junction & Altrincham Railway and from the Great Central. *Medina* is seen here at Newport in 1926.

The exterior of Freshwater station. The enamel sign proclaims Southern Railway, but closer examination of the notice boards indicates that this photograph was taken in BR days.

On 1 August 1923 independent existence came to an end and the railway became part of the Southern Railway. Unable to compete with bus and car competition, the line closed entirely on 20 September 1953. Yarmouth station is seen shortly before closure.

The Isle of Wight Steam Railway was set up in 1971 with the purchase of the 1½-mile line between Wootton and Havenstreet. Since then the line has been extended to Smallbrook, where a new junction station was constructed to enable exchange with the Island Line trains. In July 2015 Ivatt 2MT No. 41298 stands at Havenstreet with a train for Smallbrook. (Simon Burchell)